ΛNGELS

ANGELS

NANCY GRUBB

A TINY FOLIO™
Abbeville Press Publishers
New York London Paris

FRONT COVER: Detail of Lorenzo Lotto (c. 1480–1556), *Madonna and Child with Saints Catherine and James*, c. 1527–33. See page 288. BACK COVER: Detail of Giotto (1266/67–1337), *The Flight into Egypt*, c. 1305–13. See page 190. SPINE: *Angels from "Notre Dame de la Belle Verrière*," c. 1180. Chartres Cathedral, Chartres, France. See page 102. FRONTISPIECE: Detail of Rogier van der Weyden (1399/1400–1464), *The Annunciation*, c. 1435. See page 58. PAGE 6: Detail of Studio of Fra Angelico, *Adoration of an Angel*, 1st part of 15th century. Tempera on wood, 14⅜ x 9⅛ in. (37 x 23 cm). Musée du Louvre, Paris. PAGE 18: *Archangel Raphael*. Naples, Italy, late 16th century. Polychromed wood, 70 x 39⅜ in. (177.8 x 100 cm). Los Angeles County Museum of Art; Purchased with funds given by Anna Bing Arnold. PAGE 47: Detail of Sandro Botticelli (1445–1510), *The Annunciation*, c. 1489–90. See page 64. PAGE 92: Guariento di Arpo (c. 1338–1377). *Enthroned Angels*, 1354. Oil on board, 46¾ x 42 in. (119 x 107 cm). Musei Civici, Padua, Italy. PAGE 152: Detail of Raphael (1483–1520), *Madonna del Baldacchino*, c. 1507. See page 208. PAGE 222: Domenico da Tolmezzo (1448–1507). *Angel Armed with Sword*, n.d. Oil on canvas. Museo Civico, Udine, Italy. PAGE 271: Guariento di Arpo (c. 1338–1377). *Angel*, 1354. Wood, 32¼ x 19¾ in. (82 x 50 cm). Musei Civici, Padua, Italy.

EDITORS: Nancy Grubb and Mary Christian
DESIGNER: Tania Garcia
PRODUCTION EDITOR: Owen Dugan
PRODUCTION MANAGER: Lou Bilka
PHOTO RESEARCHER: Kim Sullivan

First edition
2 4 6 8 10 9 7 5 3
Library of Congress Cataloging-in-Publication Data
Grubb, Nancy.
Angels / Nancy Grubb.
p. cm.
"A Tiny folio."
Includes indexes.
ISBN 0-7892-0025-2
1. Angels. 2. Angels in art. I. Title.
BT966.2.G75 1995
235'.3—dc20
95-22219

CONTENTS

INTRODUCTION

I saw a myriad host
Of angels, festive all, with wings unfurled,
Each one distinct in brightness and in kind.
Dante, *Paradiso*, canto 31

Theologians, mystics, and poets have argued for centuries over what angels look like and even whether they can be seen at all. Thomas Aquinas, writing about angels with a philosopher's precision during the thirteenth century, declared them to be pure intellect and hence without any physical form. But for artists, angels must be made visible, and the conventions for depicting them have evolved as art and society have changed over the millennia.

Images of winged beings — man, woman, and beast —can be found in many ancient cultures. Some of the most familiar of these "proto-angels" are the monumental winged figures on Assyrian palaces, wall paintings of various Greco-Roman spirits (page 8), and particularly the goddess of Victory portrayed in classical sculpture (page 9). In some cases the differences between such prototypes and the later Judeo-Christian angels are greater than the similarities. The lightly draped Victories, for example, are all unabashedly female, whereas angels were predominantly envisioned as asexual, androgynous, or male until the nineteenth century.

Winged Spirit. Roman, 3d quarter of 1st century B.C.
From the villa of Publius Fannius Sinistor, Pompeii. Painted
mural, 49⅝ x 28 in. (126 x 71 cm). Musée du Louvre, Paris.

The Winged Victory of Samothrace, c. 190 B.C.
Marble and limestone, height: 129 in. (328 cm).
Musée du Louvre, Paris.

Angels come in many categories, and much confusion has developed regarding the names, functions, and characteristics of the different types. One often-cited source is Dionysius the Areopagite's *Celestial Hierarchy,* written about A.D. 500, in which he identifies nine orders of angels. These can be grouped into three ranks (or choirs) in descending order of power: (1) seraphim, cherubim, and ophanim (also known as thrones and often portrayed as flaming wheels); (2) dominions, powers, and authorities; and (3) principalities, archangels, and angels. Thomas Aquinas later illuminated this three-part hierarchy by assigning each rank a certain relationship to God and man. The first rank is dedicated to face-to-face worship of God; the second rank to knowing God through contemplation of the universe; and the third to human affairs. Within that third rank, the principalities watch over nations; the archangels interact with humans in extraordinary circumstances; and the angels function as guardians to individuals.

Artists—especially in the Middle Ages, when angels were newly popular in art and before certain visual conventions had been established—often found more explicit guidance from such written reports of angels than from the work of other artists, to which they had limited access. Vivid descriptions of angels appear in the Old and New Testaments but are even more plentiful in the traditional Legends of the Saints and in the Apocrypha (ancient religious texts accepted by the early church fathers and the Roman Catholic church as Holy Scripture but ultimately excluded from both the Hebrew and the Protestant canons). Particularly notable for their elaborate details are the biblical Book of Revelation and the noncanonical Book of the Secrets of Enoch (believed to be a compilation of texts written by several authors during the last two centuries B.C.). The latter is said to chronicle the patriarch Enoch's observations of heaven, where he encountered

> the archangels who are above angels . . . and the angels who are appointed over seasons and years, the angels who are over rivers and sea, and who are over the fruits of the earth, and the angels who are over every grass, giving food to all, to every living thing, and the angels who write all the souls of men . . . ; in their midst are six Phoenixes and six Cherubim and six six-winged ones continually with one voice singing one voice. (The Secrets of Enoch 19:3)

Although many incidents from the Bible and the Apocrypha were originally known primarily to literate and learned monks, certain episodes eventually became familiar to all worshipers, and these scenes became essential elements first of church decoration and illuminated manuscripts, then later of freestanding works of art. Some of these subjects provided especially apt occasions for painting angels, such as the Sacrifice of Isaac, Daniel in the Lions' Den, the Annunciation, the Nativity, the Resurrection of Christ, the Assumption of the Virgin, and the Last Judgment. Angels also play a prominent role in Islamic scripture, and artists who belonged to the Shiite branch of Islam, which did not prohibit the representation of human form, depicted angels in scenes such as the *Ascension of Muhammed on Buraq, His Mule, Guided by the Angel Gabriel* (page 283).

Dante's *Divine Comedy* (c. 1308–21) and, much later, John Milton's *Paradise Lost* (1667) also conjured up elaborate visions of angels (and fallen angels) that became part of the vernacular and inspired generations of artists. By the time the Romantic poet Lord Byron wrote his satiric *Vision of Judgment* (1821), about the arrival of King George III in heaven, angels had become nearly a cliché:

> 'Twas the archangel Michael; all men know
>> The make of angels and archangels, since
> There's scarce a scribbler has not one to show,
>> From the fiends' leader to the angels' prince;
> There also are some altar-pieces, though
>> I really can't say that they much evince
> One's inner notions of immortal spirits;
> But let the connoisseurs explain *their* merits.

Conventions for portraying angels were slow to develop and, once established, were slow to change. Certain elements became codified, offering an easy way to identify the named angels in any given scene. For example, the archangel Gabriel carries a staff or a lily when making his annunciatory visit to the Virgin Mary but a trumpet when heralding the Last Judgment; Michael almost invariably brandishes a sword with which to battle the forces of evil.

Angel imagery has steadily progressed over the centuries from the ethereal to the fleshy, paralleling Western culture's progression from faith in the unseen to reliance on direct observation and documentation. Even the early Florentine artist Giotto, who was such a pivotal figure in the transition from the medieval to the modern, still portrayed many of his angels as only quasiphysical, with their lower halves delineated more as disembodied suggestions of flight than as flesh and blood. (See, for example, the angel in the section on Joachim's dream in the Arena Chapel, page 180.) As Renaissance artists became increasingly dedicated to depicting the natural world accurately, angels became more and more three-dimensional—no longer the flat, almost translucent creatures of medieval art. Compare, for example, Simone Martini's fourteenth-century *Annunciation* (page 49) with the fifteenth-century one by Filippo Lippi (page 62), noting how the angels are situated in their surroundings.

Medieval angels were frequently placed flat against an unmodulated surface that was often painted gold to signify heavenly light. Starting in the Renaissance, angels were shown in more detailed and more convincingly familiar backgrounds, such as the Virgin Mary's book-filled bedroom or a grassy, flower-bedecked paradise. By the Baroque period, angels had become not only recognizably human but even sensual, with their wings and bodies painted or sculpted in caressingly explicit detail.

After the eighteenth century, it seemed that the less wholeheartedly people believed in angels, the more believably they were portrayed. The trend toward this paradoxically realistic depiction of angels eventually became a source of contention between the nineteenth-century Realist Gustave Courbet and the proto-Impressionist Edouard Manet regarding the latter's painting *Christ with Angels* (opposite). Courbet was known for his fierce advocacy of uncompromising realism in art. "Art in painting consists only of representations of objects visible and tangible to the artist," he wrote. "An *abstract* object, not visible, not existing, is not within the realm of painting." Given this unyielding stance, it is not surprising that Courbet greeted Manet's painting of Christ and the angels with scorn, despite the fact that its unromanticized corpse and unidealized angels had scandalized contemporary critics.

EDOUARD MANET (1832–1883).
Christ with Angels, 1864.
Graphite, watercolor, gouache, and pen and india ink on paper,
12⅝ x 10⅝ in. (32 x 27 cm). Musée d'Orsay, Paris.

As their colleague Pierre-Auguste Renoir recounted, Courbet mockingly asked Manet, "So you have seen angels then and know that they have backsides?" Edgar Degas later added: "Courbet said that never having seen angels, he did not know whether they had backsides and that, given their size, the wings Manet gave them could not have carried them. But I don't give a d—— about any of this."

By the time such irreverent comments could be made, the potential for sincere renditions of angels in the traditional mode had nearly vanished. What prevailed instead were winged figures—no longer really angels—that stood for something other than purely heavenly beings in allegories such as Jean-Auguste-Dominique Ingres's *Victoria* (opposite) and Augustus Saint-Gaudens's *Charity* (page 40).

Yet even in the late twentieth century, people continue to express faith in angels, and artists continue to portray them, as shown by Keith Haring's hovering cartoonlike being (page 44), Dorothea Tanning's surreal angelic landscape (page 310), and Komar and Melamid's radiant archangel for a church in New Jersey (page 79). These and other contemporary images communicate a sense of continuity with tradition and a spirit of aesthetic conviction that suggest that the angel may remain an eternal element in art.

JEAN-AUGUSTE-DOMINIQUE INGRES (1780–1867).
Victoria, detail of *The Apotheosis of Homer,* 1827.
Oil on canvas. Musée Bonnat, Bayonne, France.

ANGEL PORTRAITS

And I saw another mighty angel come down from heaven, clothed with a cloud: and a rainbow was upon his head, and his face was as it were the sun, and his feet as pillars of fire.

Revelation 10:1

Most angels are nameless, identified in art only by attributes such as color, clothing, or wing configuration. John Milton, in book 6 of *Paradise Lost,* suggests that angels preferred such anonymity:

> Angels, contented with their fame in Heaven,
> Seek not the praise of men.

Early Christian images of angels are so idealized that the result is a generic type rather than an individualized portrait. They usually are clad in simple robes of one or two colors, with their wings providing the only elements of decoration. But even from the beginning, a few angels were singled out for special treatment. They had names—the most familiar and the most frequently portrayed being the archangels Gabriel, Michael, and Raphael. (Gabriel and Michael are the only two angels mentioned by name in the Protestant Bible; Raphael makes an appearance in the apocryphal Book of Tobit.)

They were often lavishly costumed, with princely or ecclesiastical garb that grew more and more ornate as the centuries progressed. And they played major roles in scenes illustrating familiar stories from the Bible or from the Apocrypha.

Gabriel was the bearer of tidings both good and bad: he brought Mary news of Christ's impending birth, but he also announced the end of the world. Considered to be one of the seven angels of the Apocalypse (although not identified as such in the Book of Revelation), he sometimes holds the trumpet with which he is to sound the arrival of the final days (page 36).

Michael—often dressed in armor and bearing an unsheathed sword—was a warrior angel who led the battle against Satan. Known in the Old Testament and elsewhere as the prince of angels, he is shown as a formidable adversary. Joan of Arc declared that it was Michael who called her to do battle for France. In scenes of the Day of Judgment, he may also carry the scales of justice, with which he weighs souls to determine if they will go to heaven or to hell.

GIOTTO (1266/67–1337).
Detail of *The Ognissanti Madonna*, c. 1310.
Tempera on wood, 130 x 80¼ in. (325 x 204 cm), overall.
Galleria degli Uffizi, Florence.

Angel with Millstone, c. 1020.
Illuminated manuscript,
11½ x 8 in. (29.5 x 20.4 cm).
Staatsbibliothek, Bamberg, Germany.

Duccio di Buoninsegna (active c. 1255–1319).
Detail of *The Rucellai Madonna*, 1285.
Tempera on wood, 14 ft. 7½ in. x 9 ft. 5 in. (4.5 x 2.9 m), overall.
Galleria degli Uffizi, Florence.

GUARIENTO DI ARPO (c. 1338–1377).
Angel, 1354.
Panel, 35⅜ x 19¾ in. (90 x 50 cm). Musei Civici, Padua, Italy.

GUARIENTO DI ARPO (c. 1338–1377).
Angel, 1354.
Panel, 35⅛ x 22⅛ in. (90 x 57 cm). Musei Civici, Padua, Italy.

GIUSTO DE MENABUOI (14th century).
Saint Matthew, c. 1376.
Fresco. Baptistery of the Cathedral, Padua, Italy.

PIERO DELLA FRANCESCA (active 1439–d. 1492).
Detail of *The Madonna del Parto,* mid-1450s(?).
Fresco, 102 x 80 in. (260 x 203 cm), overall.
Cappella del Cimitero, Monterchi, Italy.

Angels, c. 1180.
Stained glass.
Chartres Cathedral, France.

RAPHAEL (1483–1520).
Detail of *The Saint Nicholas Altarpiece,* c. 1500–1501.
Oil on wood, 12⅝ x 10⅝ in. (32 x 27 cm), overall.
Pinacoteca Civica Tosio-Martinengo, Brescia, Italy.

Balls from Ecclesiastical Oil Lamps,
late 17th–early 18th century.
Ceramic, diameter (left ball): approximately 4⅜ in. (12 cm).
Musée Arménien de France, Paris.

MASTER OF AVIGNON.
Archangel Gabriel, detail of *The Annunciation,* 14th century.
Panel. Christie's, London.

MASOLINO DA PANICALE (c. 1383/84–1447?).
Archangel Gabriel, c. 1432.
Tempera on wood, 30 x 22⅝ in. (76 x 57 cm). National
Gallery of Art, Washington, D.C.

SANDRO BOTTICELLI (1445–1510).
The Angel of the Annunciation, c. 1495–98.
Tempera on canvas, 17⅝ x 5⅛ in. (45 x 13 cm).
Pushkin State Museum of Fine Arts, Moscow.

LORENZO DI CREDI (1459–1537).
Archangel Gabriel, detail of *The Annunciation*, c. 1475.
Oil on wood, 6⅜ x 23⅞ in. (16 x 60 cm), overall.
Musée du Louvre, Paris.

UNKNOWN ARTIST.
Weather Vane: Archangel Gabriel, c. 1840.
Painted sheet metal, 35 x 32½ x 1¼ in. (88.9 x 82.6 x 3.2 cm).
Museum of American Folk Art, New York.

GUARIENTO DI ARPO (c. 1338–1377).
Archangel Michael, 1354.
Wood, 35⅜ x 22¼ in. (90 x 58 cm). Musei Civici, Padua, Italy.

Archangel Michael, 14th century.
Icon. Serbisches Kloater Hilander, Berg Athos, Greece.

Saint Michael, 19th century.
Silver, approximately 7⅞ x 5⅞ in. (20 x 15 cm).
Musée Arménien de France, Paris.

Augustus Saint-Gaudens (1848–1907).
Charity, 1885. Bronze, 103⅜ x 50 x 11¾ in. (264 x 127 x 30 cm).
Musée d'Orsay, Paris.

WILLIAM WETMORE STORY (1819–1895).
Angel of Grief, 1905.
Protestant Cemetery, Rome.

EMMA STEBBINS (1815–1882).
Angel of the Waters, constructed 1868, unveiled 1873.
Bronze, height of angel: 94½ in. (240 cm).
Central Park, New York.

ABBOTT HANDERSON THAYER (1849–1921).
Winged Figure, 1889.
Oil on canvas, 51½ x 37¾ in. (131 x 96 cm).
The Art Institute of Chicago.

KEITH HARING (1958–1990).
Untitled, 1982.
Vinyl ink on vinyl tarp, 72 x 72 in. (182.8 x 182.8 cm).
Private collection, Berlin.

FRED SMITH (1886–1976).
Angel, 1950–68.
Glass-covered concrete. Fred Smith's
Wisconsin Concrete Park, Phillips.

HEAVENLY MESSENGERS

Behold, I bring you good tidings of great joy.
Luke 2:10

Angels are first and foremost messengers; in fact, the word *angel* is derived from the Greek word for messenger. One of the most frequently painted scenes in Christian art—particularly favored during the Renaissance—is the Annunciation. As chronicled in the Gospel of Luke, it was Gabriel who announced to the Virgin Mary that she would give birth to the child of God. In many Annunciations a ribbonlike banner unfurls, emblazoned with the words *Ecce ancilla domini* ("Behold the handmaid of the Lord"), taken from Luke's account.

The moment portrayed is Mary's conception by means of the Holy Spirit, which is often depicted as a beam of light streaming down from a dove. The beam frequently is directed toward her ear, embodying the medieval idea that Mary conceived through that route. Portrayals of her response to Gabriel's news became increasingly human over the centuries, progressing from the early images of a shy young woman expressing either mild surprise or calm acceptance to the decidedly alarmed maiden in Dante Gabriel Rossetti's *Ecce Ancilla Domini!* (page 77).

Gabriel is often shown as a sweet-faced, almost

feminine youth with intricately feathered wings, as in the images of the Annunciation by Fra Angelico (pages 55–57) and Rogier van der Weyden (page 58). Sometimes he hovers just above the ground—as in the Rossetti painting, where he is wingless, with flames around his feet—but more often he kneels in motionless silence, holding out a staff or a lily, the latter a symbol of the Virgin's purity.

The Nativity is also heralded by angels—in this case, an angelic choir that brings the news of Christ's birth to nearby shepherds. Most often the angels sing their praise of the event from the heavens, but sometimes they are shown as having descended to earth to worship the newborn Christ in his manger, as in the Nativities by Hugo van der Goes (page 86) and Philippe de Champaigne (page 91).

SIMONE MARTINI (c. 1283–1344)/LIPPO MEMMI (1371–1347).
Detail of *The Annunciation and Two Saints*, 1333.
Tempera on wood, 72⅜ x 82⅝ in. (184 x 210 cm), overall.
Galleria degli Uffizi, Florence.

GIUSTO DE MENABUOI (14th century).
The Annunciation, 1376–78.
Baptistery of the Cathedral, Pisa, Italy.

LORENZO MONACO (c. 1370–1422/25).
Detail of *The Annunciation with Saints Catherine,
Anthony Abbot, Procolo, and Francis,* c. 1410.
Tempera on wood, 81½ x 90 in. (207.2 x 228.8 cm), overall.
Galleria dell'Accademia, Florence.

The Annunciation.
Stained glass.
Chartres Cathedral, 1194–1220.
Chartres, France.

DONATELLO (1386–1466).
The Annunciation, late 1420s.
Gilded and polychromed *pietra di macigno*,
165 x 108 in. (419.1 x 274.3 cm).
Santa Croce, Florence.

FRA ANGELICO (c. 1400–1455).
The Annunciation, detail of *Panel with Nine Scenes from
the Silver Chest of Santissima Annunziata*, c. 1450.
Tempera on wood, each scene: 15⅛ x 15⅜ in. (39 x 39 cm).
Museo di San Marco, Florence.

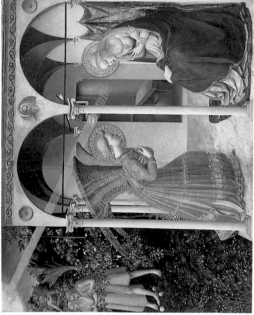

FRA ANGELICO (c. 1400–1455).
Detail of *The Annunciation*, 1435–45.
Tempera on wood, 76⅞ x 76⅞ in. (194 x 194 cm), overall.
Museo del Prado, Madrid.

FRA ANGELICO (c. 1400–1455) and workshop.
The Annunciation, late 1430s–early 1440s.
Fresco, 73⅝ × 65⅜ in. (187 × 157 cm), overall.
Monastery of San Marco, Florence.

ROGIER VAN DER WEYDEN (1399/1400–1464).
The Annunciation, c. 1435.
Wood, 33⅞ x 36⅝ in. (86 x 93 cm).
Musée du Louvre, Paris.

BENVENUTO DI GIOVANNI GUASTA (1436–1518).
The Annunciation, 1466.
Tempera on wood, 71¼ x 88¼ in. (181 x 224 cm).
Pinacoteca Comunale, Volterra, Italy.

GIOVANNI DI PAOLO DI GRAZIA (c. 1400–1482).
The Annunciation, c. 1445.
Wood, 15¾ x 18¼ in. (40 x 46 cm).
National Gallery of Art, Washington, D.C.

FRA FILIPPO LIPPI (c. 1406–1469).
The Annunciation, c. 1440.
Tempera on wood, 69 x 72 in. (175.3 x 183 cm).
Martelli Chapel, San Lorenzo, Italy.

SANDRO BOTTICELLI (1445–1510).
The Annunciation, c. 1489–90.
Tempera on wood, 59 x 61⅜ in. (150 x 156 cm).
Galleria degli Uffizi, Florence.

GIOVANNI CIMA DA CONEGLIANO (1459/60–1517/18).
The Annunciation, c. 1492.
Tempera and oil on canvas, 54 x 42 in. (137 x 106.7 cm).
The Hermitage Museum, Saint Petersburg, Russia.

LEONARDO DA VINCI (1452–1519) and others.
The Annunciation, c. 1472–75.
Oil on wood, 38½ x 85½ in. (98 x 217 cm).
Galleria degli Uffizi, Florence.

JAN PROVOST (1465–1520).
Abraham, Sarah, and the Angel, n.d.
Oil on wood, 29½ x 22 in. (75 x 56 cm).
Musée du Louvre, Paris.

GAROFALO (1481–1559).
The Annunciation, 1550.
Tempera on wood, 98⅜ x 65 in. (250 x 165 cm).
Pinacoteca di Brera, Milan.

GAROFALO (1481–1559).
The Annunciation, n.d.
Oil on wood, 21⅝ x 30 in. (55.2 x 76 cm).
Galleria degli Uffizi, Florence.

ANDREA DEL SARTO (1486–1530).
The Annunciation, 1512.
Oil on wood, 71¾ x 69¼ in. (182 x 176 cm).
Galleria Palatina, Palazzo Pitti, Florence.

The Annunciation, 14th century.
Stained glass. Milan Cathedral.

GUILIO CESARE PROCACCINI (1574–1625).
The Annunciation, c. 1610.
Oil on canvas. City of York Art Gallery, York, England.

DANTE GABRIEL ROSSETTI (1828–1882).
"Ecce Ancilla Domini!" (The Annunciation), 1850.
Oil on canvas, mounted on wood,
28⅜ x 16¼ in. (72.6 x 41.3 cm). Tate Gallery, London.

JAMES TISSOT (1836–1902).
The Annunciation, c. 1886–96.
Watercolor and gouache on paper, 6¾ x 8½ in. (17 x 21.6 cm).
The Brooklyn Museum.

KOMAR (b. 1943) and MELAMID (b. 1945).
The Annunciation, 1990. Steel, water, oil, and gold leaf,
approximately 108 x 48 in. (274.3 x 121.9 cm).
Courtesy of Ronald Feldman Fine Arts, New York.

THE NATIVITY

The Nativity, 11th century.
Icon or illumination.
Palatine Library, Parma, Italy.

TADDEO GADDI (active c. 1325–d. 1366).
The Annunciation to the Shepherds, c. 1328–30. Fresco.
Baroncelli Chapel, Santa Croce, Florence.

The Nativity, c. 1450.
Illuminated manuscript.
Christie's, London.

The Annunciation to the Shepherds, 1450.
Illuminated manuscript (cod. 1929, fol. 40).
Nationalbibliothek, Vienna.

The Nativity, c. 1450.
From a Flemish Book of Hours.
Page: 7 x 4¾ in. (17.5 x 12 cm).
Christie's, London.

SANDRO BOTTICELLI (1445–1510).
Mystic Nativity, c. 1500.
Tempera on canvas, 49¼ x 29½ in. (108.5 x 75 cm).
The National Gallery, London.

HUGO VAN DER GOES (c. 1440–1482).
Portinari Altarpiece, 1475.
Oil on wood, 99½ x 119⅝ in. (253 x 304 cm).
Galleria degli Uffizi, Florence.

MAESTRO ESIGUO.
The Nativity, 15th century.
Tempera on wood, 35⅜ x 21⅝ in. (90 x 55 cm).
Musée des Beaux-Arts, Rouen, France.

JACOPO BASSANO (c. 1510–1592).
The Annunciation to the Shepherds, c. 1533.
Oil on canvas, 45⅛ x 37 in. (116 x 94 cm).
Belvoir Castle, Leicestershire, England.

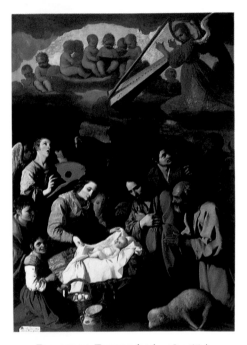

FRANCISCO ZURBARÁN (1598–1664).
The Adoration of the Shepherds, 1638–39.
Oil on canvas, 105 x 72¾ in. (267 x 185 cm).
Musée des Beaux-Arts, Grenoble, France.

PHILIPPE DE CHAMPAIGNE (1602–1674).
The Nativity, 1643.
Oil on canvas, 81½ x 45⅝ in. (207 x 116 cm).
Musée des Beaux-Arts, Lille, France.

And there are three hundred angels very bright, who keep the garden, and with incessant sweet singing and never-silent voices serve the Lord throughout all days and hours.

Book of the Secrets of Enoch 9:1

Artists reveled in the opportunity to portray large groups of angels, finding an infinite number of ways to enliven and vary such scenes. Sometimes groups of angels are clustered around a heavenly throne, as in Cimabue's *Madonna and Child in Majesty Surrounded by Angels* (page 95) and Stefan Lochner's *Virgin in a Rose Arbor* (page 141). At other times they are celebrating the Ascension of the resurrected Christ into heaven, as in Giotto's gold-brightened fresco in the Arena Chapel (page 97).

And often these angelic bands are making music. The Book of the Secrets of Enoch (17:1) provides a supposedly eyewitness account of one session of celestial music-making:

In the midst of the heavens I saw armed soldiers, serving the Lord, with tympana and organs, with incessant voice, with sweet voice, with sweet and incessant voice and various singing, which it is impossible to describe, and which astonishes every mind, so wonderful and marvelous is the singing of those angels, and I was delighted listening to it.

Such musical angels are particularly associated with scenes of paradise, either in connection with the Assumption of the Virgin or with the Last Judgment, as shown in Fra Angelico's circle of angels decorously dancing in heaven (page 103). The delineation of the horns, harps, and other instruments in these unearthly scenes is often painstakingly precise, and has provided invaluable information to researchers of early music.

Some accounts hold that angels, being made of light themselves, were brought into existence on the very first day of creation, when God separated light from darkness—an event recalled by Giusto de Menabuoi's *Creation of the World* (page 99). Early artists trying to represent angels as creatures of light often clad them in white or gold, as in the dazzling mosaics that decorate the interior dome of the Baptistery in Florence (page 106), where all nine categories of angels can be seen in marvelous detail.

CIMABUE (c. 1240–after 1302).
Madonna and Child in Majesty Surrounded by Angels, c. 1270(?).
Wood, 14 ft. x 9 ft. 3 in. (4.27 x 2.8 m). Musée du Louvre, Paris.

GIOTTO (1266/67–1337).
The Ascension, c. 1305–13. Fresco.
Arena Chapel, Padua, Italy.

GIUSTO DE MENABUOI (14th century).
Seven Angels Carrying Seven Cups, c. 1376.
Fresco. Baptistery of the Cathedral, Padua, Italy.

GIUSTO DE MENABUOI (14th century).
The Creation of the World, c. 1376.
Fresco. Baptistery of the Cathedral, Padua, Italy.

TADDEO GADDI (active c. 1325–d. 1366) and others.
Details of *The Crucifixion* and *The Ascension*, c. 1330–35.
Fresco. Sacristy of Santa Croce, Florence.

Angels from "Notre Dame de la Belle Verrière," c. 1180.
Stained glass, height: 94½ in. (240 cm).
Chartres Cathedral, Chartres, France.

FRA ANGELICO (c. 1400–1455).
. *Heaven*, detail of *The Last Judgment*, early 1430s.
Tempera on wood, 41⅜ x 82⅝ in. (105 x 210 cm), overall.
Museo di San Marco, Florence.

WORKSHOP OF FRA ANGELICO.
Madonna della Stella, 1435.
Tempera on wood, 23⅝ x 11¾ in. (60 x 30 cm).
Museo di San Marco, Florence.

Interior of the dome of the Baptistery, mid-13th century.
Mosaic. Florence.

LUCA DELLA ROBBIA (1400–1482).
The Nativity, n.d. Glazed terra-cotta.
National Gallery of Art, Washington, D.C.

LUCA DELLA ROBBIA (1400–1482). *The Resurrection*, 1442–45.
Glazed terra-cotta, 78¾ x 104¼ in. (200 x 265 cm).
Duomo, Florence.

Christ Surrounded by Cherubim, Carrying His Mother's Soul.
Berry, France, 15th century.
Marble, height: 22⅛ in. (57 cm). Musée du Louvre, Paris.

UNKNOWN ENGLISH OR FRENCH ARTIST.
The Wilton Diptych (right panel), c. 1395.
Oak, 18 x 11½ in. (45.7 x 29.2 cm). The National Gallery, London.

BENOZZO GOZZOLI (1421–1497).
Adoring Angels, detail of *The Journey of the Magi,* 1459–61.
Fresco, length: approximately 24 ft. 7 in. (7.5 m), overall.
Chapel of the Palazzo Medici-Riccardi, Florence.

ANDREA MANTEGNA (c. 1431–1506).
The Assumption of the Virgin, 1450.
Fresco. Ovetari Chapel, Church of the Eremitani, Padua, Italy.

DOMENICO GHIRLANDAIO (1449–1494).
Details of *Christ in Glory,* 1492.
Tempera on wood, 114¼ x 74¾ in. (294 x 190 cm), overall.
Pinacoteca Comunale, Volterra, Italy.

SANDRO BOTTICELLI (1445–1510).
Madonna and Child Attended by Four Angels and Six Saints, c. 1487.
Tempera on wood, 105½ x 110¼ in. (268 x 280 cm).
Galleria degli Uffizi, Florence.

MASTER OF UPPER RHINELAND.
Detail of *The Virgin in the Garden of Paradise,* early 15th century.
Städelsches Kunstinstitut, Frankfurt, Germany.

117

The Annunciation: Archangel Gabriel, 1465.
From *The Hours of Charles of France.*
Colors and gold on vellum, 6¾ x 4⅞ in. (17 x 12.4 cm).
The Metropolitan Museum of Art, New York.

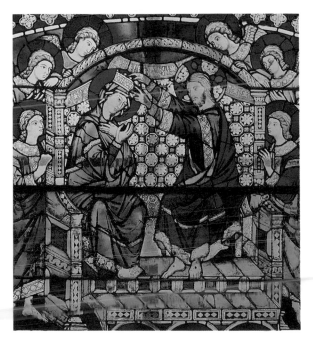

The Coronation of the Virgin, n.d.
Stained glass.
Location unknown.

Two Angels.
French, 15th century. Stained glass. Location unknown.

Saint Francis Surrounded by Angels, last half of 13th century.
Icon. Santa Maria degli Angeli, Assisi, Italy.

GIOVANNI BATTISTA MORONI (c. 1520–1578).
Details of *The Assumption of the Virgin,* c. 1550.
Oil on canvas, 141¾ x 90½ in. (360 x 230 cm), overall.
Pinacoteca di Brera, Milan.

BARTOLOMÉ ESTEBÁN MURILLO (1617/18–1682).
The Angels' Kitchen, 1646.
Oil on canvas, 5 ft. 11 in. x 15 ft. 9 in. (1.8 x 4.8 m).
Musée du Louvre, Paris. See also pages 126–27.

WILLIAM BOUGUEREAU (1825–1905).
The Virgin with Angels, 1900.
Oil on canvas, 114¼ x 74¾ in. (290 x 190 cm).
Musée du Petit Palais, Paris.

EVELYN DE MORGAN (1855–1919).
Our Lady of Peace, n.d.
Oil on canvas.
De Morgan Foundation, London.

Angels Dancing in Front of the Sun. Italian, 15th century.
Oil on wood, 22⅜ x 25⅝ in. (57 x 65 cm).
Musée Condé, Chantilly, France.

STEFANO DA VERONA (c. 1375–1451).
Angel Musicians, 14th century.
Tempera on wood. Museo Correr, Venice.

FRA ANGELICO (c. 1400–1455).
Detail of *The Coronation of the Virgin*, c. 1430–38.
Wood, 83¾ x 87⅜ in. (213 x 222 cm), overall.
Musée du Louvre, Paris.

FRA ANGELICO (c. 1400–1455).
Detail of *The Linaiuoli Triptych,* commissioned 1433.
Tempera on wood, 102⅜ x 129⅞ in. (260 x 330 cm), overall.
Museo di San Marco, Florence.

NERI DI BICCI.
The Coronation of the Virgin, 14th century.
Oil on wood, 63 x 69 in. (160 x 175 cm).
Musée du Petit Palais, Avignon, France.

BENVENUTO DI GIOVANNI GUASTA (1436–1518).
Detail of *The Ascension of the Virgin,* 1466.
Tempera on wood, entire predella: 15¾ x 88¼ in. (40 x 224 cm).
Pinacoteca Comunale, Volterra, Italy.

UNKNOWN ARTIST or MASTER OF THE LINDAU LAMENTATION.
A Choir of Angels, n.d.
Oil on gilded wood, 19½ x 12½ in. (49.5 x 32 cm).
Christie's, London.

DOMENICO GHIRLANDAIO (1449–1494).
Details of *The Adoration of the Magi,* 1488.
Tempera on wood, 112¼ x 94½ in. (285 x 240 cm), overall.
Ospedale degli Innocenti, Florence.

JAN VAN EYCK (c. 1390–1441) and HUBERT VAN EYCK (d. 1426).
Singing Angels, detail of *The Ghent Altarpiece,* c. 1432.
Oil on wood, 11 x 15 ft. (3.4 x 4.6 m), overall.
Saint Bavo, Ghent, Belgium.

STEFAN LOCHNER (c. 1400–1451).
The Virgin in a Rose Arbor, c. 1440.
Wood, 67⅜ x 48 in. (171 x 122 cm).
Wallraf-Richartz Museum, Cologne, Germany.

HANS MEMLING (c. 1430/40–1494).
Madonna and Child with Angels, c. 1480.
Wood, 23⅛ x 18⅞ in. (59 x 48 cm).
National Gallery of Art, Washington, D.C.

ALBRECHT DÜRER (1471–1528).
Detail of *Madonna of the Rose Garlands,* c. 1506.
Oil on wood, 64 x 75½ in. (162 x 192 cm), overall.
National Gallery, Prague.

MASTER OF THE SAINT LUCY LEGEND (active 1480–89).
Mary, Queen of Heaven, c. 1485.
Oil on wood, 85 x 73 in. (215.9 x 185.4 cm).
National Gallery of Art, Washington, D.C.

MELOZZO DA FORLI (1438–1494).
Music-Making Angel with Violin, c. 1480.
Fresco, 44½ x 36 in. (113 x 91 cm).
The Vatican Museums and Galleries, Rome.

PERUGINO (c. 1450–1523).
Angel Musicians, detail of *The Vallombrosa Altar*, 1500.
Galleria dell'Accademia, Florence.

RIDOLFO GHIRLANDAIO (1483–1561).
Details of *The Coronation of the Virgin*, 1504.
Oil on wood, 108⅜ x 75⅝ in. (276 x 192 cm), overall.
Musée du Petit Palais, Avignon, France.

GIOVANNI MARTINI (d. 1535).
Musical Angels, c. 1530.
Oil on wood. Museo Civico, Udine, Italy.

WILLIAM H. JOHNSON (1901–1970).
Swing Low, Sweet Chariot, c. 1944. Oil on board, 28½ x 26½ in.
(72.4 x 67.3 cm). National Museum of American Art,
Smithsonian Institution, Washington, D.C.

CHERUBS

A cherub is not a cupid, although they often look much the same; in fact, in purely visual terms, they are frequently indistinguishable. But their meanings are as different as spirituality and sexuality.

Cupid, the Roman god known as Eros to the Greeks, is a symbol of sensual love. Portrayed as a male child or adolescent, he often carries a bow and arrow, which are emblems of love's power; he is also frequently blindfolded, because love is blind. A cherub, however, has quite another meaning. Cherubim (the original plural form of *cherub*) rank as the second highest group in the celestial hierarchy and are the first angels mentioned in the Bible: in Genesis cherubim with a flaming sword guard the Tree of Life in the Garden of Eden.

In Byzantine and medieval European art cherubim often are shown as little more than stylized circle faces with four wings; even in Lucas Cranach I's sixteenth-century painting of the Trinity (page 162) the streams of cherub faces are more diagrammatic than illusionistic. With the move toward classicism and more overt eroticism in the Renaissance, and even more with the sensuality of the Baroque, they gradually evolved into the playful young cherubs seen in works by Peter Paul Rubens (page 178) and Anthony Van Dyck (page 179). Cherubs rarely wear anything more than flowers, and the form they take is that of *putti* (Italian for "little boys")—the plump, rosy-bottomed male figures used as decorative elements in both religious and mythological art. Some particularly playful butterfly-winged *putti* can be seen in Andrea Mantegna's frescoes in the Camera degli Sposi (pages 156–57).

Adoring cherubs often worship the young Christ, as in Raphael's famous *Sistine Madonna* (page 166). Paintings of the Virgin, either on earth or in heaven, frequently emphasize her role as heavenly mother by incorporating scores of cherubs, sometimes with bodies, sometimes merely winged heads. Occasionally, as in Andrea del Sarto's *Assumption of the Virgin* (page 168), they seem to be playing around her feet like restless children. By the nineteenth century, cherubs often appeared in the company of young women as symbols of their innocence (page 185). They were, at that point, very far removed from the armed cherubim of Genesis.

FRA FILIPPO LIPPI (c. 1406–1469).
Madonna and Child, c. 1465.
Tempera on wood, 37½ x 24½ in. (95 x 62 cm).
Galleria degli Uffizi, Florence.

ANDREA MANTEGNA (1431–1506).
Detail of ceiling from the Camera degli Sposi, c. 1474.
Fresco. Palazzo Ducale, Mantua, Italy.

ANDREA MANTEGNA (1431–1506).
Putti Holding Dedicatory Tablet, from the Camera degli Sposi,
c. 1474. Fresco. Palazzo Ducale, Mantua, Italy.

ANDREA MANTEGNA (1431–1506).
Madonna and Child with Cherubs, n.d.
Tempera on wood, 34⅝ x 27½ in. (88 x 70 cm).
Pinacoteca di Brera, Milan.

BENVENUTO DI GIOVANNI GUASTA (1436–1518).
Detail of *Stories of the Virgin,* c. 1470.
Tempera on wood, 71¼ x 74 in. (181 x 188 cm), overall.
Pinacoteca Comunale, Volterra, Italy.

PERUGINO (c. 1450–1523).
Virgin Enthroned with Angels and Saints, 1500.
Tempera on wood, 94½ x 55 in. (240 x 140 cm).
Galleria dell'Accademia, Florence.

LUCAS CRANACH I (1472–1553).
The Trinity, n.d.
Oil on wood, 55 x 39 in. (140 x 99 cm).
Museum der Bildenden Künste, Leipzig, Germany.

MARCO BASAITI (c. 1470–1530).
Details of *Madonna and Child with Saints,* n.d.
Oil on wood, 28⅜ x 35 in. (72 x 89 cm), overall.
Musei Civici, Padua, Italy.

RAPHAEL (1483–1520).
The Sistine Madonna, 1513.
Oil on canvas, 102⅜ x 78¾ in. (260 x 200 cm).
Staatliche Kunstsammlungen, Dresden, Germany.

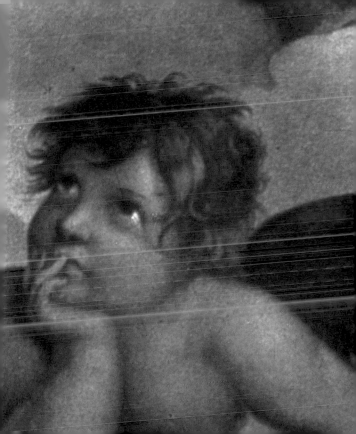

ANDREA DEL SARTO (1486–1530).
Details of *The Assumption of the Virgin,* mid-1520s.
Oil on wood, 149¼ x 87½ in. (379 x 222 cm), overall.
Galleria Palatina, Palazzo Pitti, Florence.

ROSSO FIORENTINO (1495–1540).
Musical Angel, c. 1522.
Tempera on wood, 15¼ x 18½ in. (39 x 47 cm).
Galleria degli Uffizi, Florence.

MORETTO DA BRESCIA (c. 1498–1554).
Detail of *The Glorified Virgin and Saints,* n.d.
Oil on canvas, 100⅜ x 72¾ in. (255 x 185 cm), overall.
Pinacoteca di Brera, Milan.

AGNOLO BRONZINO (1503–1572).
Detail of *The Deposition of Christ* (replica), c. 1560.
Oil on wood and fresco.
Chapel of Eleonora of Toledo, Palazzo Vecchio, Florence.

BERNARDINO LANINO (1512–1583).
Detail of *Madonna and Child with Saints*, n.d.
Oil on wood, 89¾ x 52 in. (228 x 132 cm), overall.
Pinacoteca di Brera, Milan.

173

GIOVANNI BUSI CARIANI (c. 1485–1550).
Madonna and Child with Saints, n.d.
Oil on canvas, 106¼ x 82⅝ in. (270 x 210 cm).
Pinacoteca di Brera, Milan.

GIAN PAOLO CAVAGNA (1556–1627).
Detail of *The Feeding of the Five Thousand,* n.d.
Wood, 112½ x 76 in. (286 x 193 cm), overall.
Christie's, London.

JAN BRUEGEL I (1568–1625)
and PETER PAUL RUBENS (1577–1640).
Detail of *The Virgin and Child with Fruit and Flowers,* n.d.
Oil on wood, 31⅛ x 25⅝ in. (79 x 65 cm), overall.
Museo del Prado, Madrid.

JAN BRUEGEL I (1568–1625).
Detail of *The Holy Family with the Infant Saint John*, n.d.
Copper, 6¾ x 8¾ in. (17 x 22.5 cm), overall.
Christie's, London.

PETER PAUL RUBENS (1577–1640).
Christ and Saint John with Angels, n.d.
Oil on canvas, 37½ x 48 in. (95 x 122 cm).
Wilton House, Wiltshire, England.

ANTHONY VAN DYCK (1599–1641). Detail of *The Rest on the Flight into Egypt (Virgin with Partridges)*, c. 1630.
Oil on canvas, 84⅜ x 112⅛ in. (215 x 285.5 cm), overall.
The Hermitage Museum, Saint Petersburg, Russia.

ANTONIO MARIA VIANI (called Vianino) (1555/60–1629).
Trinity with Saints Ursula and Margaret, 1619.
Oil on wood. Palazzo Ducale, Mantua, Italy.

GUIDO RENI (1575–1642).
The Coronation of the Virgin, 1626.
Oil on brass, 28⅜ x 20⅝ in. (73 x 52.5 cm).
Musée Bonnat, Bayonne, France.

GIAMBATTISTA TIEPOLO (1696–1770).
The Immaculate Conception, n.d.
Oil on canvas, 147 x 72⅜ in. (373 x 184 cm).
Museo Civico d'Arte e Storia, Vicenza, Italy.

FRANÇOIS BOUCHER (1703–1770).
The Rest on the Flight into Egypt, c. 1737.
Oil on canvas, 55 x 58½ in. (140 x 148.6 cm).
The Hermitage Museum, Saint Petersburg, Russia.

WILLIAM BOUGUEREAU (1825–1905).
Innocence, 1890.
Oil on canvas, 47 x 28 in. (119.5 x 71 cm).
Christie's, London.

PATTERNS OF FLIGHT

*And when they went, I heard the noise of their
wings, like the noise of great waters, as the voice of
the Almighty, the voice of speech, as the noise of an
host: when they stood, they let down their wings.*

Ezekiel 1:24

As intermediaries between heaven and earth, angels re-
lied on their wings to carry them swiftly from one world
to the other. Once faith in the mysterious workings of
the cosmos (angels were once believed to be responsible
for the rotation of all the celestial bodies) began to give
way to reliance on the scientific investigation of natural
laws, artists started to describe the flight of angels with
increasing literalness.

Surprisingly, until the fourth century angels were
shown wingless, but once wings started to appear, angels
often were portrayed as mostly wings and very little
body. In medieval paintings and manuscript illumina-
tions, the number (and often the color) of wings for
each type of angel was very explicitly indicated. Seraphim, for instance, were consistently identified by their
six red wings, a configuration based on Isaiah's vision in
the Old Testament:

Above it stood the seraphims: each one had six wings; with twain he covered his face, and with twain he covered his feet, and with twain he did fly.

(Isaiah 6:2)

Giotto's myriad angels in the Arena Chapel (pages 189–93) are irrepressibly acrobatic, swooping in from all directions, either solo or in battalions. As the Renaissance progressed and artists mastered the skills needed to convey convincing illusions, angels became more heavily lifelike and hence needed commensurately more substantial wings to loft them. Looking for believable models, artists studied the movement of birds, particularly those with muscular wings, such as swans and geese. At the same time, artists became ever more inventive and even whimsical in depicting the mechanics of flight, as in Braccesco's fifteenth-century *Annunciation* (page 205), where the angel appears to be surfboarding on its own halo. Views from behind or beneath airborne angels became favorite pictorial devices (see pages 214–17), and flight no longer seemed an act innate to an incorporeal spirit but rather the sometimes strained effort of a weighty body.

GIOTTO (1266/67–1337).
Detail of *Joachim's Dream*, c. 1305–13.
Fresco. Arena Chapel, Padua, Italy.

GIOTTO (1266/67–1337).
Detail of *The Flight into Egypt,* c. 1305–13.
Fresco. Arena Chapel, Padua, Italy.

GIOTTO (1266/67–1337).
Detail of *The Presentation at the Temple*, c. 1305–13.
Fresco. Arena Chapel, Padua, Italy.

GIOTTO (1266/67–1337).
Detail of *The Crucifixion*, c. 1305–13.
Fresco. Arena Chapel, Padua, Italy.

GIOTTO (1266/67–1337).
Detail of *The Lamentation*, c. 1305–13.
Fresco. Arena Chapel, Padua, Italy.

193

GIUSTO DE MENABUOI (14th century).
The Angel with Seven Cups for the Scourges, c. 1376–78.
Fresco. Baptistery of the Cathedral, Padua, Italy.

ANDREA DA FIRENZE (active 1337–77).
Detail of *Christian Learning*, c. 1365–67.
Fresco. Spanish Chapel, Santa Maria Novella, Florence.

ANTONIO DEL POLLAIOLO (c. 1432–1498).
Angel, 1467. Fresco and oil.
Chapel of the Cardinal of Portugal,
San Miniato al Monte, Florence.

AGNOLO GADDI (active c. 1370–d. 1396).
Detail of *The Dream of Heraclius,* 1380.
Fresco. Santa Croce, Florence.

Flying Angel, 15th century.
Polychromed wood, length: 21¼ in. (54 cm).
Musée du Louvre, Paris.

BENOZZO GOZZOLI (1421–1497).
Adoring Angels, detail of *The Journey of the Magi,* 1459–61.
Fresco, length: approximately 24 ft. 7 in. (7.5 m), overall.
Chapel of the Palazzo Medici-Riccardi, Florence.

PERUGINO (c. 1450–1523).
Detail of *The Virgin and Child*, c. 1500–1503. Wood, 44½ x 25¼ in.
(113 x 64 cm), overall. The National Gallery, London.

PERUGINO (c. 1450–1523).
Detail of *The Saint Augustine Polyptych*, c. 1470.
Fresco. Galleria Nazionale dell'Umbria, Perugia, Italy.

BENVENUTO DI GIOVANNI GUASTA (1436–1518).
Detail of *The Nativity*, c. 1470.
Tempera on wood, 71¼ x 74 in. (181 x 188 cm), overall.
Pinacoteca Comunale, Volterra, Italy.

DOMENICO GHIRLANDAIO (1449–1494).
Detail of *Christ in Glory*, 1492.
Tempera on wood, 114¼ x 74¾ in. (294 x 190 cm),
overall. Pinacoteca Comunale, Volterra, Italy.

CARLO DI BRACCESCO (active 1478–1501).
The Annunciation, n.d. Wood, center panel of triptych:
62¼ x 42¼ in. (105 x 52 cm). Musée du Louvre, Paris.

ALBRECHT ALTDORFER (c. 1480–1538).
The Birth of Mary, c. 1525. Oil on canvas,
55½ x 51½ in. (141 x 131 cm). Alte Pinakothek, Munich.

RAPHAEL (1483–1520).
Madonna del Baldacchino, c. 1507.
Oil on wood, 109 x 88¼ in. (277 x 224 cm).
Galleria Palatina, Palazzo Pitti, Florence.

PAOLO VERONESE (1528–1588).
Detail of *The Wife of Zebedee Interceding with
Christ over Her Sons,* n.d.
Oil on canvas, 141¾ x 71 in. (360 x 180 cm), overall.
Burghley House, Stamford, England.

FEDERICO BAROCCI (c. 1535–1612).
Detail of *The Circumcision,* 1590.
Oil on canvas, 130¼ x 98¾ in. (356 x 251 cm), overall.
Musée du Louvre, Paris.

PETER PAUL RUBENS (1577–1640).
Detail of *The Gonzaga Family in Adoration of the Holy Trinity*, n.d.
Oil on canvas, 71 x 43⅜ in. (180 x 110 cm), overall.
Palazzo Ducale, Mantua, Italy.

EL GRECO (1541–1614).
Detail of *The Assumption of the Virgin*, 1577.
Oil on canvas, 158 x 90 in. (401 x 229 cm), overall.
Museo de Santa Cruz, Toledo, Spain.

REMBRANDT VAN RIJN (1606–1669).
The Archangel Raphael Leaving Tobias's Family, 1637.
Oil on wood, 26 x 20½ in. (66 x 52 cm).
Musée du Louvre, Paris.

GIAMBATTISTA PIAZZETTA (1683–1754).
The Assumption of the Virgin, 1735.
Oil on canvas, 16 ft. 11 in. x 96½ in. (5.15 x 2.45 m).
Musée du Louvre, Paris.

JUAN CARREÑO DE MIRANDA (1614–1685).
Detail of *Mass for the Founding of the Trinitarian Order*, 1666.
Oil on canvas, 16 ft. 5 in. x 10 ft. 10 in. (5 x 3.3 m), overall.
Musée du Louvre, Paris.

GIAMBATTISTA TIEPOLO (1696–1770).
Detail of *The Martyrdom of Saint John of Bergamo,* n.d.
Oil on canvas. Duomo, Bergamo, Italy.

JOSEPH MALLORD WILLIAM TURNER (1775–1851).
Angel Standing in Storm, c. 1840.
Oil on canvas, 31 x 31 in. (78.7 x 78.7 cm).
Tate Gallery, London.

ODILON REDON (1840–1916).
The Winged Man or the Fallen Angel, before 1880.
Oil on cardboard, 9⅜ x 14 in. (24 x 35.5 cm).
Musée des Beaux-Arts, Bordeaux, France.

BATTLES OF GOOD AND EVIL

And there was war in heaven: Michael and his angels
fought against the dragon.

Revelation 12:7

Evil seems to be more inspiring than goodness to artists
and writers, and both have long given the devil his due.
Dante's *Inferno* and John Milton's *Paradise Lost* provided
much of the imagery adopted by visual artists in portraying scenes of the war in heaven between the rebel angels,
led by Satan, and the good angels, led by the archangel
(and later saint) Michael. This metaphoric battle between
good and evil was often depicted quite literally, with
Satan and an armor-clad, sword-wielding Michael in
armed combat. According to Milton, Satan had rebelled
at being instructed to bow down to Christ, and in resis-
tance he gathered round him a third of all the angels in
heaven. As Milton wrote in book 6 of *Paradise Lost*:

Wide was spread
That war, and various: sometimes on firm ground
A standing fight; then, soaring on main wing,
Tormented all the air; all air seemed then
Conflicting fire.

After losing the battle, the rebel angels plummeted into the depths of hell, a scene spectacularly portrayed by Pieter Bruegel I (page 233) and others.

Having originated as chief of the seraphim (the highest angelic order), Satan retained certain characteristics of angel anatomy that were perverted into devilish attributes. According to canto 34 of Dante's *Inferno*:

A wondrous thing it was to see his head,
Wearing three faces, scarlet to the fore . . .
Beneath each head two mighty wings emerged . . .
No feathers did they bear but like a bat's
Their covering was.

Sometimes Satan takes the guise of a dragon rather than a man (see pages 236, 246), but leathery wings are almost always an identifying feature, as is a serpentine tail.

The New Testament Book of Revelation, which provides the basic text for the story of the end of the world, is filled with complex and visually specific imagery. Artists were particularly inspired by the Four Horsemen (page 254) and the Seven Angels of the Apocalypse (pages 248–51). The Last Judgment—which is predicted to take place after the final battle with Satan has been won and Christ has returned to earth in triumph to judge "the quick and the dead"—was also a favored scene. Christ often is shown encircled by numerous angels, while down below devils are carrying away sinners to their eternal torment. Michael is usually there to aid in the judgment process by weighing souls (page 238), and a devil often lurks nearby—and occasionally tries to tip the scale in damnation's favor.

A few episodes in the Old and New Testaments describe conflicts between angels and humans, with angels acting in a punitive or combative rather than protective role. Particularly popular with artists were the Expulsion from Paradise, when an angel with a flaming sword drove Adam and Eve out of the Garden of Eden (pages 226–29), and Jacob's night-long fight with an unnamed angel, from whom he was determined to wrest a blessing (pages 230–31).

FRA ANGELICO (c. 1400–1455).
Detail of *The Annunciation,* 1435–45.
Tempera on wood, 76⅜ x 76⅜ in. (194 x 194 cm), overall.
Museo del Prado, Madrid.

GIUSTO DE MENABUOI (14th century).
Adam and Eve, 1376–78. Fresco.
Baptistery of the Cathedral, Pisa, Italy.

GIOVANNI DI PAOLO DI GRAZIA (c. 1400–1482).
Detail of *The Annunciation,* c. 1445.
Wood, 15¾ x 18¼ in. (40 x 46 cm), overall.
National Gallery of Art, Washington, D.C.

GIOVANNI DI PAOLO DI GRAZIA (c. 1400–1482).
The Creation of the World and the Expulsion from Paradise, c. 1445.
Tempera and gold on wood, 19 x 20½ in. (46.5 x 52 cm).
The Metropolitan Museum of Art, New York.

EDWARD STEINLE (1810–1886).
Jacob Wrestling with the Angel, 1837.
Oil on canvas. Private collection.

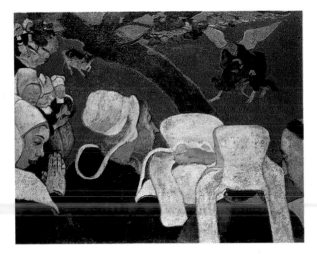

PAUL GAUGUIN (1848–1903).
Vision after the Sermon: Jacob Wrestling with the Angel, 1888.
Oil on canvas, 28⅜ x 35¾ in. (72.2 x 91 cm).
The National Gallery of Scotland, Edinburgh.

MASTER OF THE REBEL ANGELS (1st part of 14th century).
Detail of *The Fall of the Rebel Angels,* n.d.
Wood. Musée du Louvre, Paris.

PIETER BRUEGEL I (c. 1525/30–1569).
The Fall of the Rebel Angels, 1562.
Oak, 46 x 63¾ in. (117 x 162 cm).
Musée des Beaux-Arts, Brussels.

PACINO DI BONAGUIDA (14th century).
Detail of *The Apparition of Saint Michael*, c. 1340.
Tempera and gold leaf on parchment,
17¼ x 12⅝ in. (43.8 x 32.2 cm). The British Library, London.

Tattoo by Bill Baker after Martin Schoengauer's
woodcut of Saint Michael.

Saint Michael Slaying the Dragon.
French, 2d quarter of 12th century.
Stone, 33½ x 30½ x 9¾ in. (85 x 77 x 25 cm).
Musée du Louvre, Paris.

PIERO DELLA FRANCESCA (active 1439–d. 1492).
Saint Michael, c. 1460–69.
Tempera on wood, 52⅜ x 23⅜ in. (133 x 59 5 cm).
The National Gallery, London.

ROGIER VAN DER WEYDEN (1399/1400–1464).
Saint Michael Weighing Souls, detail of *The Last Judgment,* 1443.
Oil on wood, 39⅜ x 55 in. (100 x 140 cm), overall.
Musée de l'Hôtel-Dieu, Beaune, France.

RAPHAEL (1483–1520).
Saint Michael Trampling the Dragon, 1518.
Oil on canvas, 106⅜ x 63 in. (270 x 160 cm).
Musée du Louvre, Paris.

AGNOLO BRONZINO (1503–1572).
Saint Michael, 1540–46. Fresco.
Chapel of Eleonora of Toledo, Palazzo Vecchio, Florence.

EMMANUEL FREMIET (1824–1910).
Saint Michael, 1879–97.
Hammered copper, 20 ft. 3 in. x 8 ft. 6 in. x 4 ft.
(6.17 x 2.6 x 1.2 m). Musée d'Orsay, Paris.

WILLIAM BLAKE (1757–1827).
*Satan in His Original Glory: "Thou Wast Perfect
Till Iniquity Was Found in Thee,"* c. 1805.
Watercolor on paper, 16¾ x 13⅜ in. (42.9 x 33.9 cm).
Tate Gallery, London.

JEAN-JACQUES FEUCHÈRE (1807–1852).
Satan, 1834.
Bronze, 31 x 21 x 12½ in. (79 x 53 x 32 cm).
Los Angeles County Museum of Art.

THE APOCALYPSE

Detail of *War in Heaven*. Norman, c. 1320. From *The Apocalypse*.
Color, gold, silver, and brown ink on vellum,
12⅛ x 9 in. (30.7 x 23 cm), overall.
The Metropolitan Museum of Art, New York.

Detail of *Fifth Trumpet: The Plague of Locusts.* Spanish, mid-10th century. From Beatus de Liébana (d. 798), *Commentary on the Apocalypse,* and Jerome, *Commentary on Daniel.* Illuminated manuscript. The Pierpont Morgan Library, New York.

Detail of *The Sixth Angel Delivers the Four Angels That Had Been Enchained in the Euphrates.* Spanish, c. 1180. From Beatus de Liébana (d. 798), *Commentary on the Apocalypse.* Tempera and gold leaf on parchment, 17½ x 11¾ in. (44.5 x 30 cm), overall. The Metropolitan Museum of Art, New York.

Detail of *The Mission of the Seven Angels with the Seven Cups.*
Spanish, 1091–1109. From Beatus de Liébana (d. 798),
Commentary on the Apocalypse. Miniature on parchment, 9¼ x
13 in. (23.5 x 33 cm), overall. Biblioteca Nacional, Madrid.

Detail of *The Seventh Angel of the Apocalypse Proclaiming the Reign of the Lord*. Spanish, c. 1180. From Beatus de Liébana (d. 798), *Commentary on the Apocalypse*. Tempera, gold, and ink on parchment, 17½ x 11¾ in. (44.5 x 30 cm), overall. The Metropolitan Museum of Art, New York.

Saint John Takes the Book from the Seventh Angel,
detail of *The Apocalypse of Angers,* c. 1360–80.
Tapestry. Musée des Tapisseries, Angers, France.

LUCAS CRANACH I (1472–1553).
Revelations: The Seven-Headed Dragon, 1534.
Woodcut. Private collection.

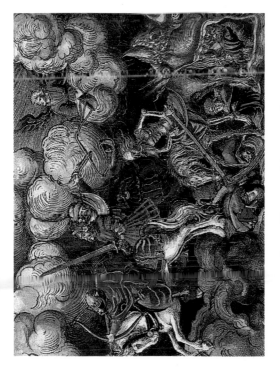

LUCAS CRANACH I (1472–1553).
The Riders of the Apocalypse, 1534.
Woodcut. Private collection.

ALBRECHT DÜRER (1471–1528).
The Riders of the Apocalypse, 1498.
Woodcut, 15⅜ x 11 in. (39.2 x 27.9 cm).

CHRISTIAN MICHAEL.
End of the World, 1992.
Oil on canvas, 36 x 38 in. (91.4 x 96.5 cm).
Ramis Barquet, Monterrey, Mexico.

Details of *The Fall of the Rebel Angels, Psalter of Blanche de Castille.*
From *Les Superstitions,* 1186.
Illuminated manuscript. Bibliothèque de l'Arsenal, Paris.

DIERIC BOUTS (c. 1415–1475).
The Fall of the Damned, c. 1450.
Oil on wood, 45¼ x 27⅜ in. (115 x 69.5 cm).
Musée des Beaux-Arts, Lille, France.

DIERIC BOUTS (c. 1415–1475).
The Way to Paradise, c. 1450.
Oil on wood, 45¼ x 27⅜ in. (115 x 69.5 cm).
Musée des Beaux-Arts, Lille, France.

HANS MEMLING (1430/40–1494).
Details of *The Last Judgment,* c. 1480. Wood.
Memling Museum, Bruges, Belgium. See also pages 264–65.

The Angel, from Charles VI Tarot Deck.
Ferrara, Italy, c. 1470–80.
Woodblock print and tempera on cardboard,
7 x 3½ in. (18 x 9 cm).
Bibliothèque Nationale de France, Paris.

Detail of *Theophany: Adoration of God in Heaven.*
Spanish, 10th century. From Beatus de Liébana (d. 798),
Commentary on the Apocalypse. Illuminated manuscript.
El Escorial, Real Biblioteca de San Lorenzo,
San Lorenzo de El Escorial, Spain.

GIOTTO (1266/67–1337).
Details of *The Last Judgment*, c. 1305–13.
Fresco. Arena Chapel, Padua, Italy.

GUARDIAN ANGELS
AND COMPANIONS

Every visible thing in this world is put under the change of an angel.
Saint Augustine (354–430), *Eight Questions*

Within the nine orders of angels, only archangels and angels (the two lowest categories in the hierarchy) are traditionally said to interact with man and woman in the course of daily life. In some cases, the angel serves only as a messenger, but in others, the angel lingers in visible form, taking responsibility for the well-being of individuals in trouble, guarding them from harm, offering them sustenance, or leading them out of danger.

The most elaborate tale is that of the blind Tobit and his son Tobias, from the apocryphal Book of Tobit. The archangel Raphael arrived, unannounced and unidentified, at Tobit's door, offering to guide Tobias on a business trip to a nearby town. Along the way, Raphael instructed Tobias to catch a large fish and preserve its gall, heart, and liver. When they arrived at their destination, Tobias learned about the travails of his cousin Sarah, who was possessed by a demon who had devoured each of her seven husbands on their wedding night. Tobias bravely married Sarah nonetheless, and at Raphael's instruction he cooked the heart and liver of the fish, whose fumes drove the demon to "the remotest parts of Egypt."

After Tobias and Sarah celebrated their good fortune, they returned to Tobit, whose blind eyes were opened—again at Raphael's instruction—once they were rubbed with the gall of the fish. This adventure-filled tale with its picturesque cast of characters, including Tobias's little dog, proved irresistible to artists ranging from Francesco Botticini (page 301) and a follower of Andrea del Verocchio (page 300) to Rembrandt (page 215).

Some Old Testament scenes of human-angel interaction particularly favored by artists include Daniel in the Lions' Den (page 274) and several events from the life of Abraham—notably, the visit of the three angels (page 276) and the Sacrifice of Isaac, when, at the last minute, an angel stayed Abraham's hand from cutting his son's throat as an offering to God (pages 278–80). The prophet Elijah is often shown being fed by an angel in the wilderness (page 285) or being lifted to heaven in a fiery chariot led by an angel (page 282).

In scenes inspired by the New Testament, angels are shown offering sustenance to the Holy Family on their flight into Egypt, which Anthony Van Dyck transformed into an image of cherubs frolicking with the young Christ (page 179). Later, an angel greeted the three Marys at the empty tomb, announcing to them that Christ had risen from the dead (page 291).

Certain characters are identifiable by their ever-present angels. Saint Matthew, one of the four Evangelists, is accompanied by an angel who dictates the Gospel to him (pages 292–95), and Saint Bernard is often portrayed with his vision of the Virgin Mary surrounded by a host of angels (pages 297–99). In Victorian times, the idea of a guardian angel became particularly associated with children and young lovers, who often are shown under the sheltering wing of increasingly feminine angels.

Detail of *Daniel in the Lion's Den*, n.d.
From Beatus de Liébana (d. 798),
Commentary on the Apocalypse. Illuminated manuscript.
The British Library, London.

Detail of *Old Testament Scene from the "Macie Jowski Bible,"* c. 1250.
Illuminated manuscript.
The Pierpont Morgan Library, New York.

GAUDENZIO FERRARI (1471/81–1546).
Abraham and the Three Angels, n.d.
Oil on canvas. Private collection.

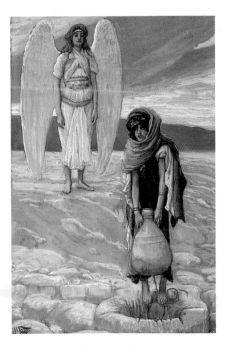

JAMES TISSOT (1836–1902).
Hagar and the Angel in the Desert, c. 1896–1900.
Watercolor on paper, 9⅜ x 6 in. (23.8 x 15.3 cm).
The Jewish Museum, New York.

FILIPPO BRUNELLESCHI (1377–1446).
The Sacrifice of Isaac, 1401–2.
Competition panel for the Baptistery doors.
Gilded bronze, 21 x 17½ in. (53.3 x 44.5 cm).
Museo Nazionale del Bargello, Florence.

LAURENT DE LA HYRE (1606–1656).
Abraham Sacrificing Isaac, 1650.
Oil on canvas, 38 x 47⅝ in. (96.4 x 121 cm).
Musée Saint-Denis, Reims, France.

REMBRANDT VAN RIJN (1606–1669).
The Sacrifice of Isaac, 1634.
Oil on canvas, 62¼ x 46 in. (158 x 117 cm).
The Hermitage Museum, Saint Petersburg, Russia.

SCHOOL OF PSKOV.
The Ascension of Elijah, 15th century. Wood.
Museum of the History of Religion, Saint Petersburg, Russia.

*The Ascension of Mohammed on Buraq, His Mule,
Guided by the Angel Gabriel.* Persian, 1539–43.
Illuminated manuscript. The British Library, London.

PETER PAUL RUBENS (1577–1640).
The Prophet Elijah Receiving Bread and Water from an Angel,
c. 1625–28. Oil on wood, 25⅜ x 21⅜ in. (65 x 55 cm).
Musée Bonnat, Bayonne, France.

JACOB JORDAENS (1593–1678).
The Flight into Egypt, c. 1640.
Oil on canvas, 39¾ x 53 in. (101 x 135 cm).
Pushkin State Museum of Fine Arts, Moscow.

HANS THOMA (1839–1924).
The Flight into Egypt, n.d.
Oil on canvas. Private collection.

287

Lorenzo Lotto (c. 1480–1556).
Madonna and Child with Saints Catherine and James, 1527–33.
Oil on canvas, 44¾ x 59¾ in. (113.5 x 152 cm).
Kunsthistorisches Museum, Vienna.

JACQUES DE STELLA (1596–1657).
Christ Served by the Angels, n.d.
Oil on canvas, 23⅝ x 31½ in. (60 x 80 cm).
Galleria degli Uffizi, Florence.

SANDRO BOTTICELLI (1445–1510).
Christ on the Mount of Olives, c. 1500.
Tempera on wood, 20¾ x 13¾ in. (53 x 35 cm).
Museo de la Capilla Real, Granada, Spain.

EDWARD BURNE-JONES (1833–1898).
The Morning of the Resurrection, 1882.
Oil on canvas, 32½ x 60 in. (82.5 x 152.5 cm).
Christie's, London.

Angel Dictating to Saint Matthew the Evangelist (from Chartres
Cathedral), 2d quarter of 13th century.
Stone, 26 x 19⅝ in. (66 x 50 cm). Musée du Louvre, Paris.

FILIPPO BRUNELLESCHI (1377–1446).
Saint Matthew, 1442–46.
Glazed terra-cotta, diameter: 67 in. (170 cm).
Pazzi Chapel, Santa Croce, Florence.

JACOPO DA PONTORMO (1494–1556).
Saint Matthew, c. 1527–28.
Oil on wood, diameter: 27½ in. (70 cm).
Capponi Chapel, Santa Felicita, Florence.

EDWARD BURNE-JONES (1833–1898).
Saint Matthew, n.d.
Oil on canvas. Roy Miles Gallery, London.

FILIPPINO LIPPI (1457/58–1504).
The Vision of Saint Bernard, mid-1480s.
Tempera on wood, 82¾ x 76¾ in. (210 x 195 cm).
Badia, Fiesole, Italy.

Fra Bartolommeo (c. 1474–probably 1517).
The Virgin Appears to Saint Bernard, c. 1504–7.
Tempera on wood, 84⅝ x 90⅞ in. (215 x 231 cm).
Galleria degli Uffizi, Florence.

FOLLOWER OF ANDREA DEL VEROCCHIO (c. 1435–1488).
Tobias and the Angel, c. 1470–80.
Egg tempera on poplar, 33 x 26 in. (83.6 x 66 cm).
The National Gallery, London.

FRANCESCO BOTTICINI (c. 1446–1497).
The Three Archangels and Tobias, c. 1470.
Tempera on wood, 60¼ x 60⅝ in. (153 x 154 cm).
Galleria degli Uffizi, Florence. See also pages 302–3.

GIANLORENZO BERNINI (1598–1680).
The Ecstasy of Saint Teresa, 1645–52.
Marble, life-size. Santa Maria della Vittoria, Rome.

WILLIAM BLAKE (1757–1827).
Angels Watching over the Tomb of Christ, c. 1806.
Watercolor on paper. Victoria and Albert Museum, London.

JAMES TISSOT (1836–1902).
Guardian Angel, n.d.
Watercolor and gouache on paper.
The Jewish Museum, New York.

M. L. MACOMBER (1861–1916).
Faith, Hope, and Charity, 1894.
Oil on canvas. Roy Miles Gallery, London.

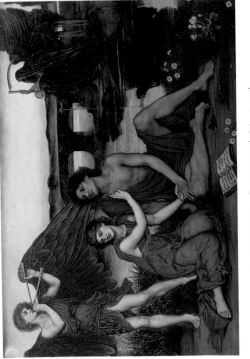

John William Godward (1861–1922).
The Betrothed, n.d.
Oil on canvas, 17¾ x 31½ in. (45 x 80 cm). Guildhall Art Gallery, London.

JOSE GARNELO ALDA (1866–1944).
The Death of Saint Francis, 1916.
Oil on canvas. Museo Provincial, Valencia, Spain.

DOROTHEA TANNING (b. 1912).
Guardian Angels, 1946.
Oil on canvas, 48 x 36 in. (122 x 91.4 cm).
New Orleans Museum of Art.

INDEX OF
DONORS' CREDITS

INDEX OF
ILLUSTRATIONS

317

PHOTOGRAPHY
CREDITS